The Official

Coloring Book

Universe

The Official Bob Ross Coloring Book

First published in the United States of America in 2017 by
UNIVERSE PUBLISHING
A division of Rizzoli International Publications, Inc.
300 Park Avenue South
New York, NY 10010
www.rizzoliusa.com

2017 2018 2019 2020 / 10 9 8 7 6 5 4 3

Design by Lynne Yeamans / Lync
Printed in the United States

ISBN-13: 978-0-7893-2772-7
Library of Congress Control Number: 2017905629

"I don't try to understand
everything in nature. I just look
at it and enjoy it..."

"...let's make some nice little clouds that just float around and have fun all day."

"There's enough unhappy
things in the world, painting
should be one of those things
that brightens your day..."

"Every painting is going to be different, and that's what makes it great."

"This is not something you should
labor over or worry about."

"You have to have dark in order to show light, just like in life."

"Now then, let's wash the
old brush, that's the fun part
of this whole technique."

"...okay, shake off the excess and
just beat the devil out of it."

"You can move mountains, rivers, trees, you can determine what your world is like..."

"These things live right in your brush, all you have to do is shake them out, there..."

"This would be a good place for
my little squirrel to live..."

"Let me extend a personal
invitation for you to drag out
your brushes and a few paints
and paint along with us..."

"Just let your imagination go.
You can create all kinds of beautiful
effects, just that easy..."

"Enjoy it. If painting does nothing else,
it should make you happy."

"We just show you how, but
you make the decisions. When you
have this much power, you have
to make big decisions..."

"Anything we don't like, we'll turn it into a happy little tree or something, because as you know, we don't make mistakes, we just have happy accidents."

"And that may be the true joy of painting, when you share it with other people. I really believe that's the true joy..."

"Did you ever think you could just
take a great big old brush and
make all these beautiful little trees?
You really can..."

"You know me, I think there ought to be a big old tree right about there. And let's give him a friend, everybody needs a friend, there..."

"Anything that you try and
you don't succeed, if you learn
from it, it's not a failure."

"Let's put a few little highlights in
here, just to make them little rascals
just sparkle in the sun..."

"And the more that you paint, the more that you're able to visualize... you really can learn to be creative as you paint. It's like anything else, it just takes a little practice."

"And success with painting leads
to success with many things, it carries
over into every part of your life."

"You have unlimited power here,
you can do that. You can do
anything on this canvas, anything..."

"Son of a gun, that's a pretty nice tree
for being done that quick..."

"Let's get crazy, what the heck.
Take a two inch brush, this is
your bravery test..."

"Isn't that fantastic?
I knew you could do it."

"I look forward to seeing you again."

"Happy Painting, God bless my friend..."